MARLEGENDS

MARLEGENDS

Zephry

Copyright © 2019 by Zephry.

ISBN: Softcover 978-1-7960-0440-3
 eBook 978-1-7960-0439-7

All rights reserved. No part of this book may be reproduced or transmitted in any form or by any means, electronic or mechanical, including photocopying, recording, or by any information storage and retrieval system, without permission in writing from the copyright owner.

Any people depicted in stock imagery provided by Getty Images are models, and such images are being used for illustrative purposes only.
Certain stock imagery © Getty Images.

Print information available on the last page.

Rev. date: 06/27/2019

To order additional copies of this book, contact:
Xlibris
1-800-455-039
www.Xlibris.com.au
Orders@Xlibris.com.au
798723

All artworks are original and created by the author.

absorbing elders

shhh muppet

im not gonna let you outta worm

climb the ladder

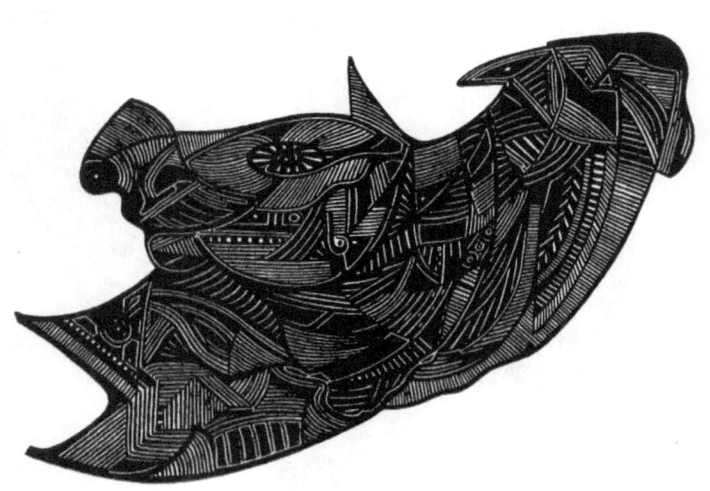

darkness is never alone

the religion of the now is cosmic

don't run away

circular doors

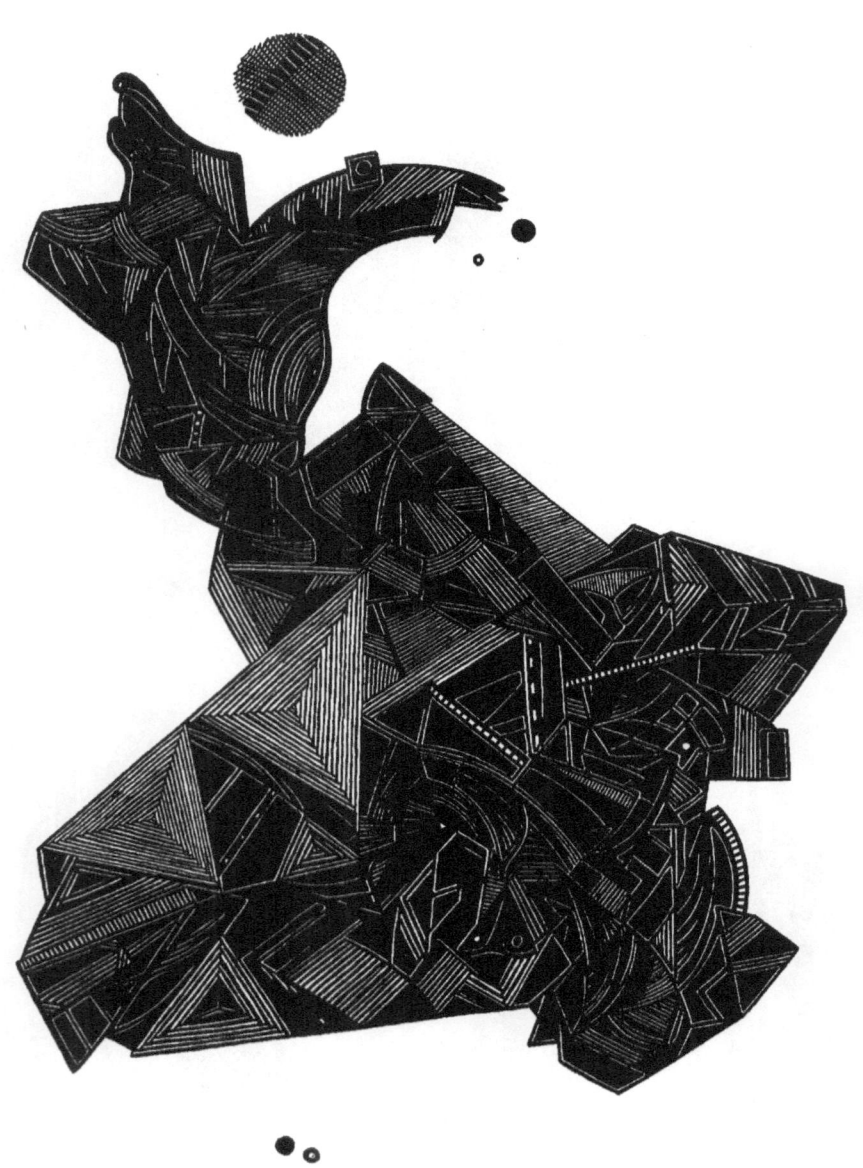

in order to find our first breath you exband

find your beat/flow

we haven't even been born yet

time is a current

one track path

time is like a dime

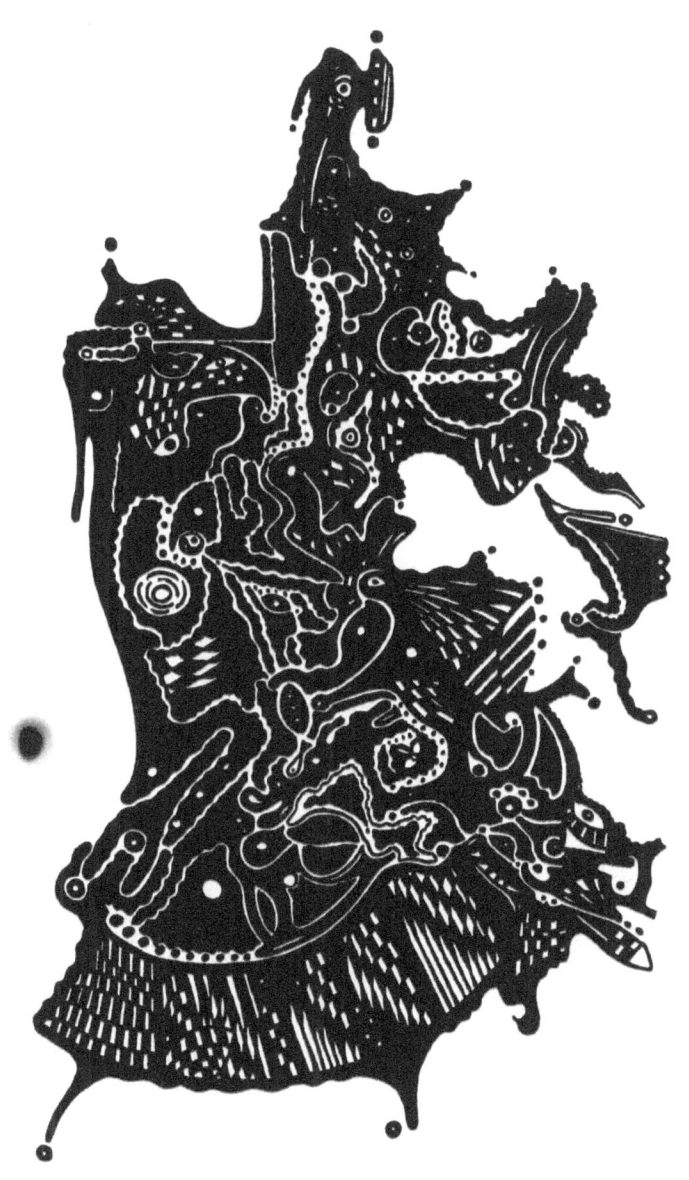

scan through toast

my point is light

men use lemons to smoke outta

jealou@

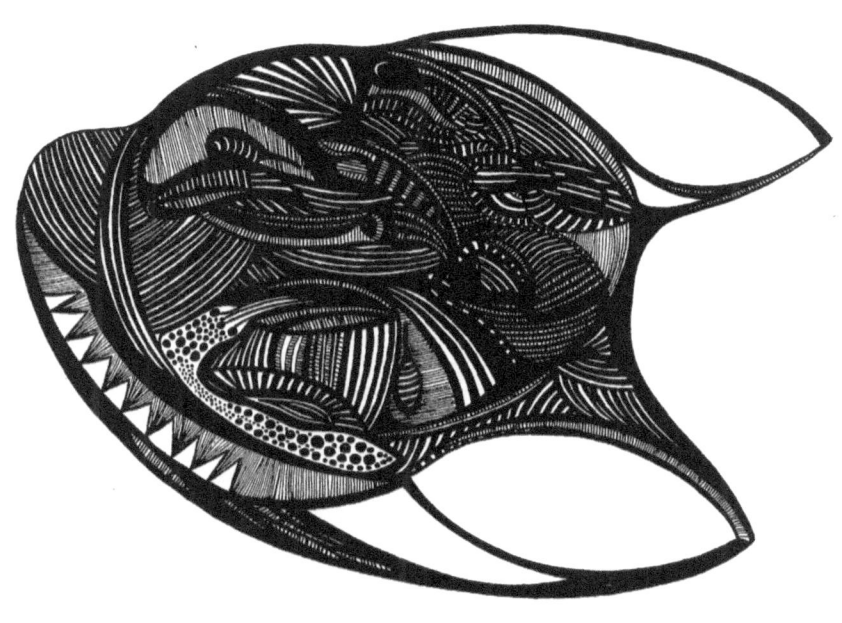

big picture

clairvoyance

my heart is heavy

my head is steady

my ears are ready

parasite

shake it out

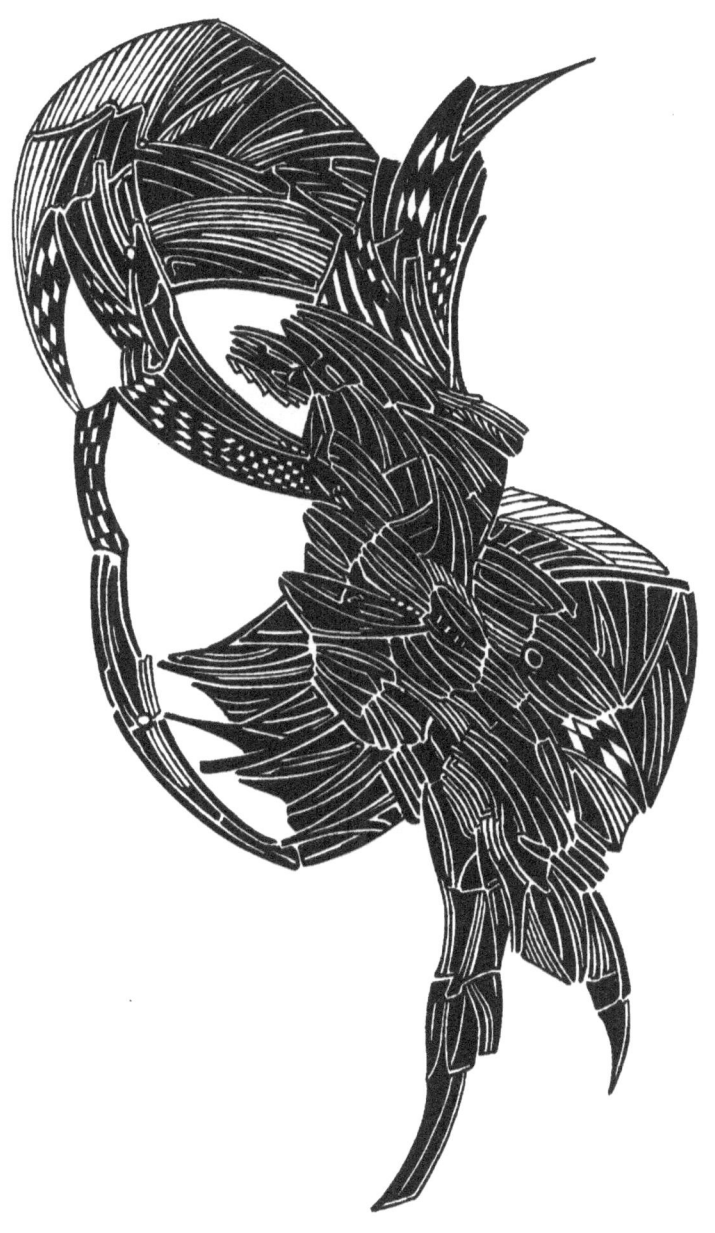

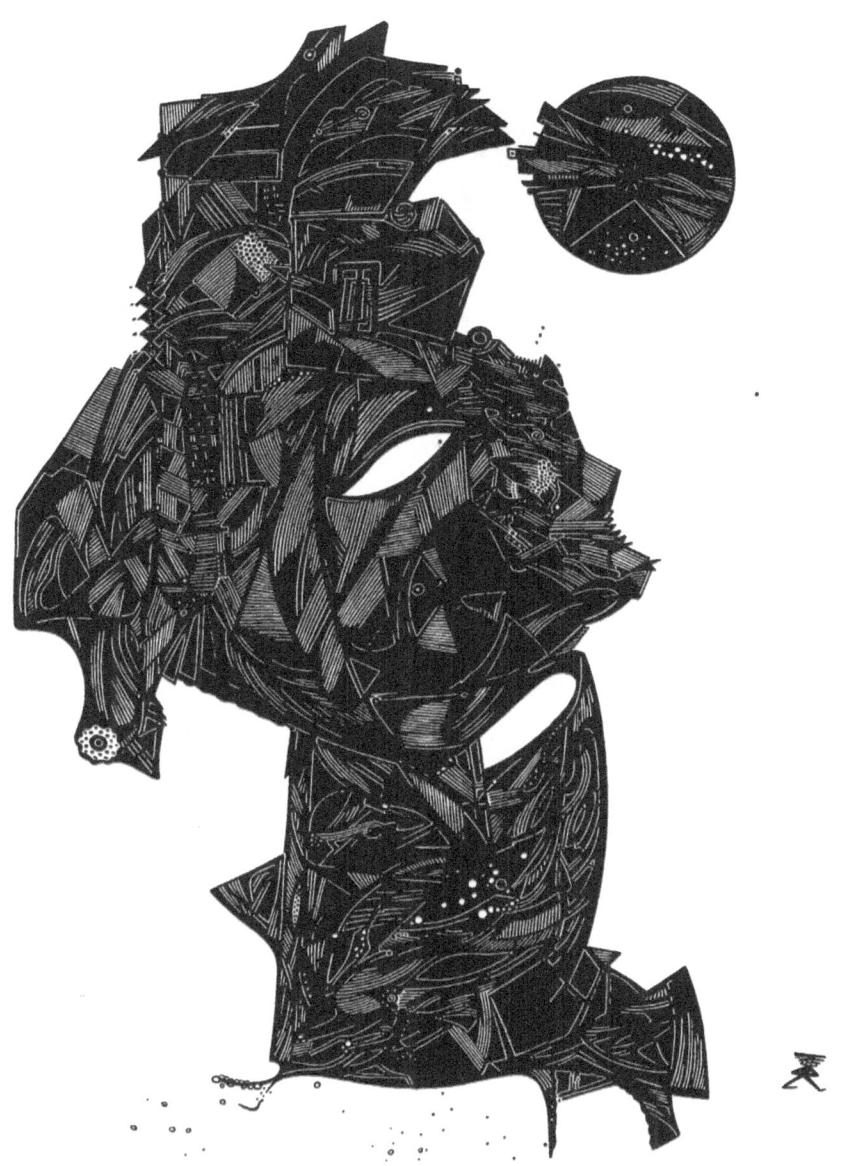

if you listen, they will guide you

www.ingramcontent.com/pod-product-compliance
Lightning Source LLC
Chambersburg PA
CBHW031503210526
45463CB00003B/1056